Looking at Minibeasts

Slugs
and Snails

Sally Morgan

Contents

Words in **bold** are
explained on page 31.

Slugs and snails

Slugs and snails are part of a group of animals called **molluscs**. Most molluscs have a **shell**.

A snail carries its shell on its back. A slug has a tiny shell hidden inside its body. Both animals glide along slowly on a large **foot**. This is a flat muscle on the underside of the slug or snail.

A snail has a hard shell and a soft body.

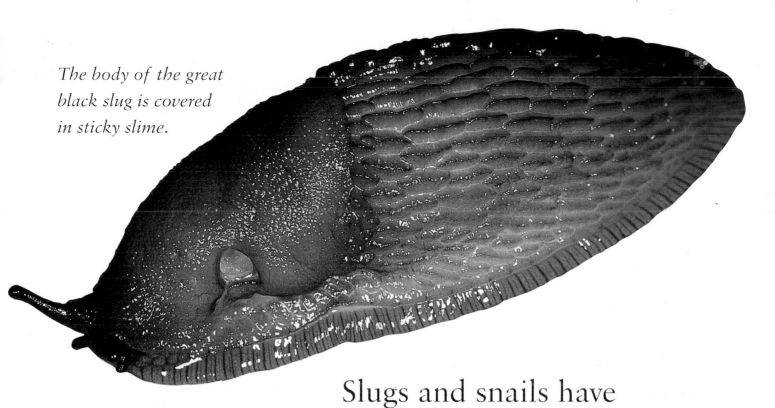

The body of the great black slug is covered in sticky slime.

Slugs and snails have two long **tentacles** and two short tentacles on their heads. The long tentacles are for seeing. The short tentacles are for smelling and tasting.

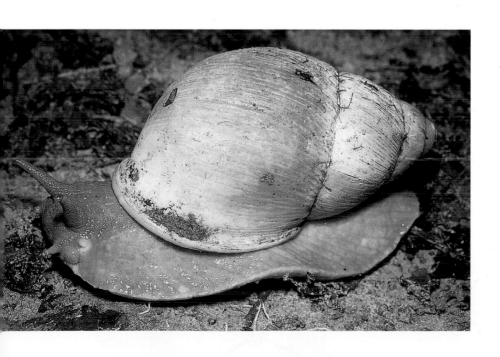

The giant snail lives in rainforests. It glides across the forest floor.

The snail family

Some molluscs live in gardens and parks, but many more live in ponds, rivers and oceans. The snail's largest relatives are squid, cuttlefish and octopuses. These molluscs live in the sea. They have long tentacles which may be covered in **suckers**. Their shells are hidden inside their bodies.

This brightly-coloured sea slug lives in water.

The cuttlefish has ten tentacles on the front of its head.

The members of the snail family vary in size. Glass snails are just a few millimetres long. The giant squid is one of the largest molluscs. It grows up to 20 metres long.

Mussels are molluscs which live on the seashore. They attach themselves to the rocks.

Living in a shell

A snail's shell is made of a hard material like chalk. The shell protects the snail's soft body. When the snail is frightened or under attack from another animal, it pulls its body into the shell. As the snail grows, it has to make more shell.

*The garden snail has a **spiral** shell which has a pattern of light and dark bands.*

A snail stretches out its body while it is moving or feeding (left).

A snail adds new material to the edge of its shell to make it larger. If the shell is a **spiral**, the spiral gets larger and larger.

If you touch a snail, it pulls its body back into its shell (above).

A hermit crab does not have a shell of its own. Instead, it lives in the shell of a dead sea snail.

9

Shell shapes

Snail shells are many shapes and sizes.

Some shells are cone-shaped. Other shells

have a spiral pattern. Mussels, scallops, oysters

and clams are molluscs that live in the sea. They

are **bivalves**. This means they have two shells

joined together. Bivalves can open and close

their shells, just like opening and closing a door.

*The conch is
a type of snail.
It has one of
the largest shells.*

This scallop is a bivalve, because it has two shells.

Shells can be many colours. Most land snails have brown shells. Sea snails often have brightly-coloured shells. Some shells have spots and stripes.

When a snail shell is cut in half, you can see a spiral which winds round and round.

Land and water

Slugs and snails like damp, shady places such as woods. Here they can hide under logs and leaves. Only a few types of slugs and snails live in the hot, dry parts of the world.

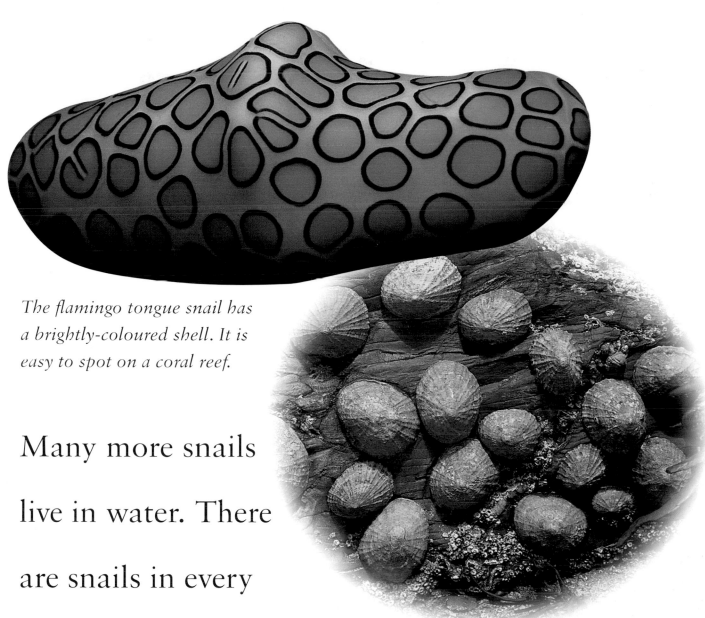

The flamingo tongue snail has a brightly-coloured shell. It is easy to spot on a coral reef.

Many more snails live in water. There are snails in every pond. Colourful tropical snails live

Limpets attach themselves to rocks on a beach. They can live underwater and out of the water.

on **coral reefs**. You can find snails on the beach too – in **rock pools** and under the sand.

Moving over land

Slugs and snails move very slowly, using a flat muscle called a foot. The foot is a large part of the body of a slug or snail. Its underside is covered in a slimy **mucus**. This helps the animal to glide over the ground.

The foot of this snail is twice as long as its shell.

*The underside of
a snail's foot is
flat and covered
in mucus.*

Everywhere they go,
snails and slugs leave
behind a shining trail
of dried mucus.

Moving in water

Pond snails use a foot to move too. They glide across the surface of the water and climb over plants. Larger molluscs move in different ways. Scallops are **bivalves** which jump across the sea bed if another animal tries to attack them.

This scallop is jumping across the sea floor.

The squid and the octopus move by shooting out a powerful jet of water. The jet pushes the animal backwards through the water.

The great pond snail (above) can grow up to 5 centimetres long.

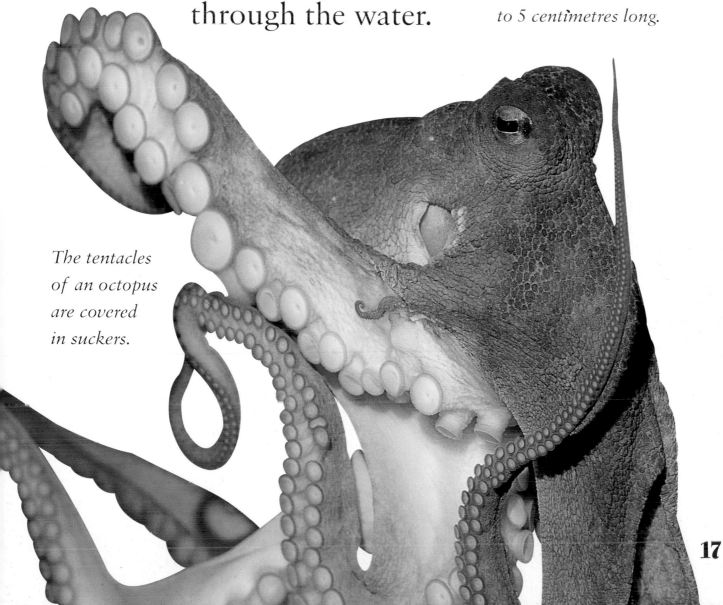

The tentacles of an octopus are covered in suckers.

Hundreds of teeth

Snails and slugs are **pests** because they like to eat young garden plants. Their tongues are covered in hundreds of teeth, which makes them rough, like sandpaper. Slugs and snails use their rough tongues to rip leaves to pieces.

This roman snail is eating a leaf by scraping its tongue over the surface.

Animals that eat plants are called **herbivores**. Most slugs and snails are herbivores, but a few are **predators**. Predators feed on other animals.

Slugs (right) eat fruits, leaves and the shoots of plants.

Dog whelks are predators. They use their tongues to drill through the shells of other snails.

Under attack

Many animals like to eat slugs and snails. The thrush catches a snail in its beak. Then it crushes the snail's shell by hitting it hard against a stone. When the shell is in pieces, the thrush can eat the soft body inside. The thrush uses the same stone again and again. Around the stone are the broken shells of all the snails it has eaten.

Sometimes snails are attacked by ants. The ants kill the snail by biting its soft body.

Sea slugs are very brightly coloured. The colours are a warning to other animals to stay away. Parts of a sea slug's body are covered with **sting cells**. The slug protects itself from predators by firing poison-tipped threads from its sting cells.

The sea slug is poisonous. Its bright colours scare off attackers.

21

Night animals

During the day, snails and slugs hide under logs, pots and stones. They come out at night when it is cooler. They like the warm, damp evenings of spring and autumn. If you go outside with a torch on a damp evening, you may see hundreds of snails looking for food.

These snails are hiding in an old plant pot during the day.

The opening of this snail's shell is sealed up with mucus.

Snails often cluster on fence posts in hot weather. They stay there until wet weather returns.

Snails may dry up in very hot weather. They seal up the opening of their shells with a thick layer of mucus. This stops water from leaving their bodies.

Finding their way

Slugs and snails use their tentacles to find their way around. A snail has two pairs of tentacles at the front of its head. The shorter pair is for tasting and smelling. Each of the long tentacles has a simple eye at the end.

Snails cannot see as well as we can, but they can **detect** light. This means that a snail can move towards or away from light.

Pond snails use their tentacles to find food in the water.

From egg to adult

Land snails lay small, white eggs in holes in the ground. They may lay as many as 40 eggs in each hole. After four weeks, tiny baby snails hatch out. They start feeding at once, and grow very quickly.

1. Snails lay tiny white eggs in the soil.

2. Miniature snails hatch from the eggs. As they grow, their shells grow too.

Pond snails lay their eggs on pond weeds. The eggs are covered in a jelly. This stops other animals from eating the eggs.

This blob of jelly contains many pond snail eggs.

3. A snail may take two years to reach adult size. Some snails live as long as ten years.

3

Watching minibeasts

Slugs and snails are found in damp, shady places – under pots, logs and stones for example. Look for them on a warm, damp evening. You can catch slugs and snails by making a trap out of a grapefruit skin.

The animals creep under the skin during the day. Trapped slugs and snails can be kept in a damp, shady fish tank. Ask an adult to help you put soil and leaves into the

To make a slug trap, rest one edge of a grapefruit skin on a stone.

tank. Then add a few moss-covered twigs and stones. Make sure the tank has a lid to stop the animals from escaping. The snails will eat leafy vegetables such as lettuce.

If you keep snails in a fish tank, put them back where you found them after a few weeks.

Snails and slugs are safe to handle. Look at them with a magnifying glass, or ask an adult to place a slug or snail on a sheet of perspex. You can watch the animal move from beneath the sheet.

You can see how snails behave in the wild by painting numbers on their shells. Then put them back in the garden. You can find out where the snails hide, how far they move, and what they like to eat.

Always ask an adult to make sure the paint is non-toxic and does not touch the snail's body.

Minibeast sizes

Slugs and snails are many sizes. The pictures in this book do not show them at their actual size. Below you can see how big they are in real life.

Garden snail shell
4 centimetres wide

Sea slug
4 centimetres long

Dog *whelk shell*
2 centimetres wide

Great black slug
up to 15 centimetres long

Glossary

bivalve A mollusc that has two shells.

coral reef A hard wall made by sea animals called coral.

detect To find out or discover.

foot The flat part of a slug or snail, used for moving around.

herbivore An animal that only eats plants.

mollusc An animal with a soft body and a shell.

mucus A thick, sticky slime.

pest An animal that damages crops.

predator An animal that hunts and eats other animals.

rock pool A pool of seawater trapped between rocks on a beach.

shell A hard outer covering.

spiral A curve that winds round and round on itself.

sting cells Parts of an animal that make poisonous stings.

suckers Round shapes on an animal's body that grip things.

tentacles The feelers of a snail, or the arms of an octopus or squid.

Index

Editor: Russell McLean
Designers: John Jamieson, Ian Butterworth
Picture researcher: Sally Morgan
Educational consultant: Emma Harvey

First published in the UK in 2000 by
Belitha Press Limited
an imprint of Chrysalis Books plc
64 Brewery Road, London N7 9NT

Paperback edition first published in 2002

ISBN 1 84138 167 5 (hardback)
ISBN 1 84138 391 0 (paperback)

Printed in Hong Kong

British Library Cataloguing in Publication Data for this book is available from the British Library.

10 9 8 7 6 5 4 3 2 1 (hardback)
10 9 8 7 6 5 4 3 2 1 (paperback)

Picture acknowledgements:
Jeff Collett/Ecoscene: 3b, 7t, 11b. Anthony Cooper/Ecoscene: 22. W. Lawler/Ecoscene: 10b. John Liddiard/Ecoscene: 6b, 16. OSF: 20. Papilio: front cover b, 2, 3t, 9b, 14, 17b, 19t, 23t, 25t, 25c. Robert Pickett/Papilio: front & back cover tcr & tr, 5t, 13t, 15r, 17t, 23b, 27t, 30. Ken Preston-Mafham/Premaphotos: front cover tcl & c, back cover tcl, 1, 4b, 5b, 8b, 9t, 9c, 11t, 12, 13c, 18, 21t, 24-25, 26bl, 26br, 27b, 30cl, 30cr. Rod Preston-Mafham/Premaphotos: front & back cover tl, 19b, 21b, 30bl, 30c. Barrie Watts: 7c, 15l.